Squid Ink Publishing™
ISBN: 979-8-9895681-0-9
Copyright © 2023 Grant Trotter & Kyle Trotter
Art and Design by Amber Gulilat

THE COLONARY ARTS

*A Bathroom
Haiku Assortment*

GRANT TROTTER
KYLE TROTTER

Art and Design by Amber Gulilat

Toilet seat found warm

Brings comfort to the body

But not to the mind

Cold porcelain blades

Strike unsuspecting hamstrings

The seat was left up

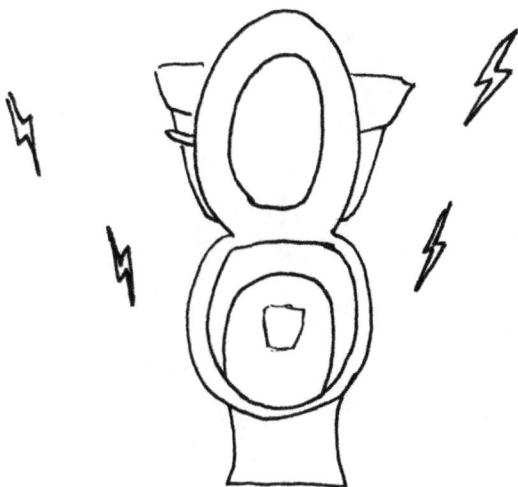

Shiny marble floor
Elegant, but reflective
Stall mates can see all

It feels a moment

But time has slipped long away

My numb legs can't stand

Plane lavatory

Painstakingly engineered

So no one can fit

My confidence wrecked

Reapproaching the table

Shoe dragging paper

Why do I only

Allow my mind to wander

While defecating?

Misaligned door frame

Lock bolt extends into air

I may have a guest

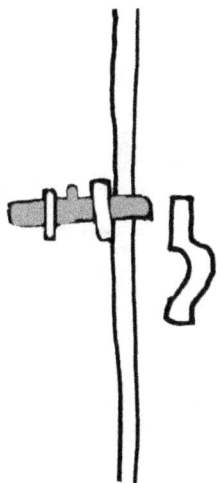

Seat covers empty

Angst sets in, hepatitis

Will soon be my friend

Feeling lonely, but
Suddenly hope for love found
Etched on partition

555-5555

CALL ME

Phone used on toilet

Another quiet moment

Deftly avoided

Touchless faucet shuns

Twenty second handwashing

Recommendation

What goes in comes out
But after much imbibing
It's through the same door

You reap what you sow

In this moment I question

My diet choices

The odor without

Betrays corruption within

Wretched man I am!

It is courtesy

Not shame, for which I conceal

My present actions

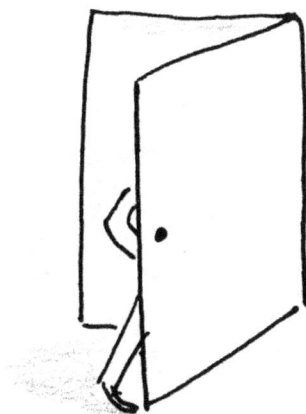

When hard seasons come

Just work smarter not harder

Utilize fiber

I must wash my hands
To make myself feel okay
About what I've done

Bam! All ears ringing

Shockwave convulses their house

Not a soft-close seat

I need to speed up

Or else everyone will know

I'm not just peeing

Bathroom attendant

Panhandler of the restroom

Avert eye contact

There's almost never

Someone behind the curtain

But you never know

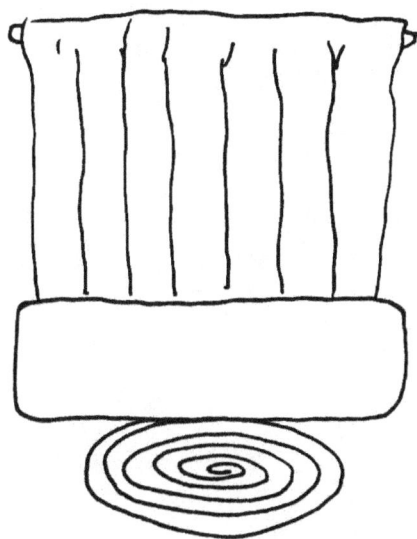

A running faucet

Provides excellent cover

When stuck at a friend's

Tiny airport stall

Must contort my suitcase in

No hope of egress

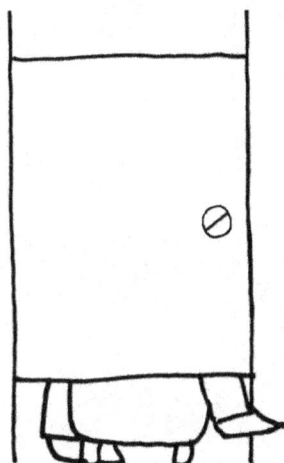

Teamwork, a fine trait

Too broadly applied in trips

To women's restroom

It's not what one eats

That defiles one's self, but lo:

It's that which comes out

Inadequately

Cultured for squat toilet shock

During distant trip

Doing the same thing
Expecting altered results
I'll wipe yet again

It's hard to feel pride

With pants around one's ankles

Forced humility

No purse hooks in sight
But the floor is unseemly
What's a girl to do?

Non-elongated

Toilet seat, rule out and find

A better bathroom

An unsought crowd lurks

With expectancy outside

Porta potty door

Cease useless straining
Strike when the iron is hot
Try again later

Single ply paper

Fold and wad with abandon

Never give up hope

Bathroom smartphone use

Unhygienic, yet simply

Irresistible

If the toilet clogs
I'll finally be exposed
As a monstrous brute

Transcending paper
Like holy water cleansing
Unholy places

Loved ones may approach

With endless needs and requests

But a poop gives rest

Stunning cinema

But bursting bladder misses

The intermission

Pondering all day

But the solution appears

At once on the throne

This wet bar of soap

Schemes yet another daring

Escape from my grasp

Deepest love is found

In the pet eagerly perched

Just outside the door

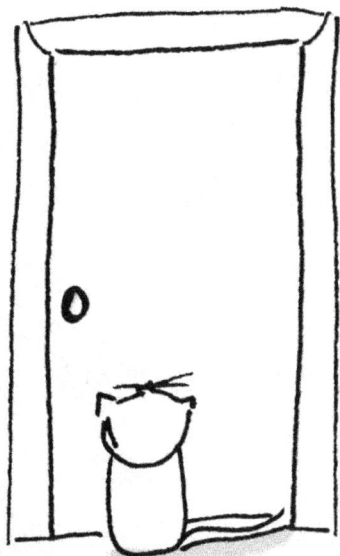

Nature is calling
But too busy to answer
I'll take my chances

A crucial work call

Such inopportune timing

Will they learn the truth?

A relaxing break

Turned to pitch-black search challenge

By motion light switch

Kids beg for rest stop

But we need to cover ground

Dare I call their bluff?

NEXT REST STOP
50 MILES

Partition walls give

A semblance of privacy

But footwear names names

When the shift drags on

The stalls tacitly become

A fleet of break rooms

This specific book

Under these circumstances

Held by others' hands

The roll is empty
If only I had realized
Two seconds sooner

ACKNOWLEDGEMENTS

Special thanks to the following people, whose enthusiasm and assistance helped make this book the best it could be:

Joel, Erica, Shayla, Kristen, Denise, Marc, Eko, Julie, Peter, David, Maggie, and Eyakem

www.ingramcontent.com/pod-product-compliance
Lightning Source LLC
Chambersburg PA
CBHW051734040426
42447CB00008B/1130